THE CURIOSITY BOX

MINIBEASTS

by Peter Riley

Illustrated by Krina Patel

W
FRANKLIN WATTS

Franklin Watts
Published in paperback in Great Britain in 2019
by The Watts Publishing Group

Credits
Series Editor: Amy Stephenson
Series Designer: Krina Patel
Illustrations: Krina Patel
Picture Researcher: Amy Stephenson /
Diana Morris

ISBN: 978 1 4451 4645 4

Printed in China

MIX
Paper from
responsible sources
FSC® C104740
www.fsc.org

Franklin Watts
An imprint of
Hachette Children's Group
Part of The Watts Publishing Group
Carmelite House
50 Victoria Embankment
London EC4Y 0DZ

An Hachette UK Company
www.hachette.co.uk

www.franklinwatts.co.uk

To Ken and Dorothy – PR

To Peter Sage – KP

Picture Credits: AFPics/Shutterstock: 22c. Aggata/Dreamstime: 25c. Anest/Dreamstime: 23cr. Anest/Shutterstock: 13tc. Arco Images/Alamy: 27tl. Aruna/Dreamstime: front cover cr, 28bl. Darins Banzys/Dreamstime: 14t. Radu Berian/Shutterstock: 20br. Graham Braid/Dreamstime: 13c. Calvste/Shutterstock: 22t. Chainphoto24/Shutterstock: 8t. Anat Chant/Shutterstock: 11tl. Riawphai Chantarachit/Shutterstock: back cover tl, 6t. Colette3/Shutterstock: 18bc. Concept Photo/Shutterstock: 23t, 29br. crazy stocker/Shutterstock: front cover cl. Dance Strokes/Shutterstock: 5tl. Evgororov/Dreamstime: 15t. Domiciano Pablo Romero Franco/Dreamstime: 17b. Kurt G/Shutterstock: 20tr. Alexander Gabrysch/Getty Images: 27cl. Ian Gowland/SPL: 11b, 28cr. Ian Grainger/Shutterstock: 25tr, 29bl. Roger Griffith/cc wikimedia commons: 21bl. Fritz Geller-Grimm/cc wikimedia commons: 11tr. Arto Hakola/Shutterstock: 18br. H Helene/Shutterstock: 24cr. italii Hulai Shutterstock:,27tr. Jdm.photos/Shutterstock: 5tr. Industry and Travel/Shutterstock: 19b, 29cr. Eric Isselee/Shutterstock: back cover cr, 15b, 16t, 29cl. Jarp2/Shutterstock: 25tl. kamnuan/Shutterstock: 15c. Mikhail Kokhanchikov/Dreamstime: 9bc. H Krisp/cc wikimedia commons: 21br. D. Kucharski K Kucharska/Dreamstime: 18t. D. Kucharski K Kucharska/Shutterstock: back cover cl, 5tc, 22b. Cheryl Kunde/Shutterstock: 24t. Henrik Larsson/Shutterstock: 6c, 9t, 10t, 10c. Hervé M/Dreamstime: 13cl. Sonja M/Shutterstock: 9br. Cosmin Manci/Dreamstime: 24br. Cosmin Manci/Shutterstock: 24cl. Meisterphotos/Dreamstime: 25br. Mirage 3/Dreamstime: 23b, 28br. Mark Mirror/Shutterstock: 18bl, 18bcl. Vladimir Mozgovay/Dreamstime: 13b. Napat/Shutterstock: front cover c. NHM/Alamy: 6b. Michael Nyvle/Dreamstime: 25bl. Jens Ottoson/Shutterstock: 17c. Marc Parsons/Dreamstime: 27br. Photofun/Shutterstock: 21tr. photowind/Shutterstock: 13tr. Pincasso/Shutterstock: 23cl. Yaroslava Polosina/Dreamstime: 5bc. Daniel Prudek/Shutterstock: 19tr. Dr Morely Read/Shutterstock: 21tl. Ian Redding/Dreamstime: 24bl. Sue Robinson/Shutterstock: 20tl. Paul Rommer/Shutterstock: 16bc, 16br. Yordan Rusev/Dreamstime: 5br. Gina Sanders Dreamstime: 13cr. Schankz/Shutterstock :9c. Scubaluna/Shutterstock: 26b, 27tc. Emjay Smith/Shutterstock: 19tc. Torbjorn Swenelius/Dreamstime: 17t. Vincius Tupinamba/Dreamstime: 5bl. Marco Uliana/Shutterstock: 10cl. Tim Heusinger von Waldegge/Dreamstime: 19tl. Tony Watson/Alamy: 7b, 28c. whiskeybottle/Dreamstime: 20bl, 21bc. Zaclurs/Dreamstime: front cover br. Evgenii Zadiraka /Shutterstock: 27clb.

CONTENTS

⚠ This symbol shows where there is some information to help you stay safe around minibeasts. Words in **bold** can be found in the glossary on page 30.

WHAT ARE MINIBEASTS?

Minibeasts are little animals. You can find them outside.
Sometimes you can even find them inside your home!

There are many curious things to discover about minibeasts in this book.

Sometimes you have to guess what you see, then turn the page to find the answer.

Near the back of this book is our minibeast curiosity box. You can talk about it with your friends.
You can make your own curiosity box about minibeasts if you visit a garden, a park or the countryside.

ARMOURED MINIBEASTS

Minibeasts are very small animals, much smaller than a cat or a squirrel. Minibeasts do not have a **skeleton** of bone inside them like you do.

Some minibeasts have their skeletons on the outside of their bodies. They are made from hard materials and they cover all of a minibeast's body, like a suit of armour. **Insects**, woodlice and spiders have this kind of skeleton.

insect (bee)

woodlouse

spider

SOFT MINIBEASTS

Some minibeasts have skeletons made of water! Earthworms and slugs have soft, damp bodies. The water inside their bodies holds them up and gives their bodies shape. **Muscles** under the soft skin use the water to help them move the minibeast's body along.

Snails have skeletons made of water too, but they also have a hard shell they can hide in.

earthworm

slug

snail

MINIBEASTS ON THE GROUND

If you are out on a walk, look at the ground or the soil in any flower bed you pass. You may see an insect called a BEETLE running along looking for food.

Most beetles have two hard, shiny WING cases along their back. They have a pair of wings under the wing cases. They use their wings to fly.

ROVE BEETLES have short wing cases. They do not cover all of the beetle's back.

A very large rove beetle is called the Devil's coach horse. If you get too close it bends up its back, makes a foul smell and can give you a painful bite!

wing case

rove beetle

Devil's coach horse

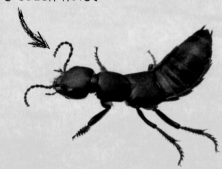

If you look very closely at the ground for a minute you may see a tiny minibeast walking or jumping about. This is a SPRINGTAIL. It has a suit of armour like a beetle.

The springtail has a **limb** like a fork under its body. It flicks this limb when it wants to jump.

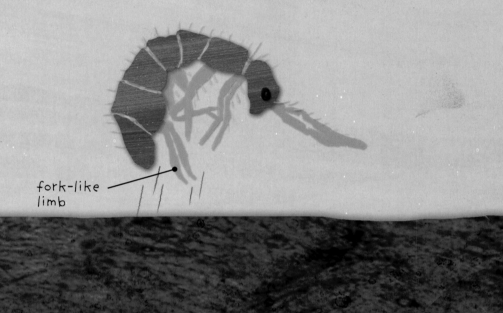

fork-like limb

WHAT CAN THIS BE?

Animal poo?
Soil that has been eaten by an animal?
An animal that looks like soil?
Turn the page to find out.

IN THE SOIL
It's soil that has been eaten by an animal!

Sometimes an earthworm leaves a curly pile of soil **grains** on the surface of the ground. They are called WORM CASTS.

EARTHWORMS make **burrows** in damp soil. They eat soil grains as they make their burrows. They feed on tiny living things that are in the soil as the grains pass through their bodies.

Worm casts are a sign that worms are living in the soil below this patch of grass.

worm cast

Earthworms come out of their burrows at night. When an earthworm finds a leaf to eat, it pulls it into its burrow.

leatherjacket larva
(see page 9)

There are many other minibeasts that live in the soil
to hide from animals that might eat them.

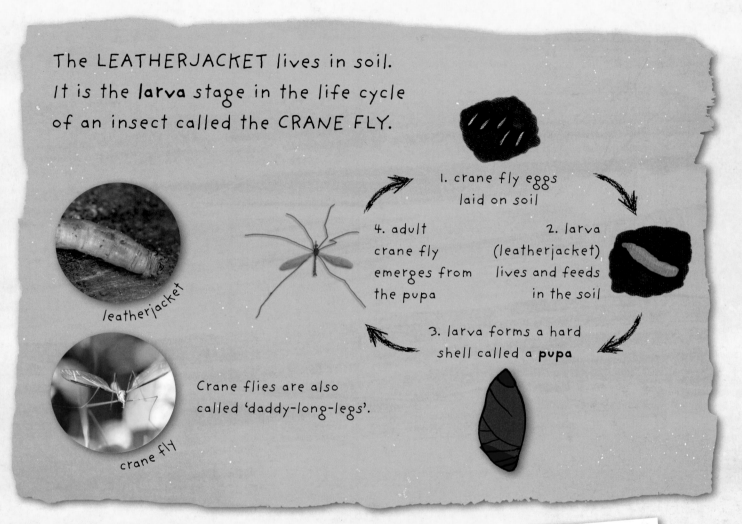

The LEATHERJACKET lives in soil.
It is the **larva** stage in the life cycle
of an insect called the CRANE FLY.

leatherjacket

crane fly

Crane flies are also
called 'daddy-long-legs'.

1. crane fly eggs
laid on soil

4. adult
crane fly
emerges from
the pupa

2. larva
(leatherjacket)
lives and feeds
in the soil

3. larva forms a hard
shell called a **pupa**

When animals like birds and
mammals die, their bodies
sometimes sink into the soil.
Some minibeasts, such as
MAGGOTS, feed on dead bodies.

Maggots are the larva stage of
a fly called the blue bottle.

blue bottle

maggot

UNDER STONES

You might find some stones at the edge of a flower bed. If you gently lift them up you may spot some minibeasts! Animals that live under stones use this damp, dark habitat during the day.

Under a stone you may find an insect called an EARWIG and even some earwig eggs. When the eggs hatch, the young earwigs stay close to their mother for safety. As they grow they **moult** their skins until they become adults.

This female earwig is guarding her nest of eggs.

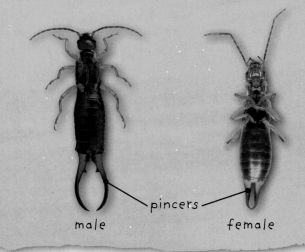

pincers

male   female

You can tell a male earwig from a female earwig by the shape of their PINCERS. A male has curved pincers and a female has straight ones.

Under another stone, see if you can spot a long, thin minibeast. It is an **arthropod** (arth-ro-pod) called a CENTIPEDE. It can run away quickly. Under its head it has a pair of poison claws. It uses them to catch other soil animals, such as small earthworms, which it eats.

poison claws

There is a strip of shiny material on the soil.
It goes under a third stone ...

WHAT CAN THIS BE?

A shiny ribbon?
A trail of water?
A trail of slime?
Turn the page to find out.

It's a trail of slime!

The slime has been made by a slug.

Slugs make SLIME in the skin of their foot and use it to slide along. When the slug has gone, the slime dries up and shines in the sunlight.

mantle

eye

long tentacle

short tentacle

slime

foot

When a slug starts to move, it pops out a pair of short **TENTACLES** to taste the ground. Next it pops out a pair of long tentacles. Each one has an eye on the end to help it see where it is going.

Slugs belong to an animal group called **molluscs**. There are many different kinds of slugs. Here are four of them.

leopard slug

grey field slugs

large black slug

red slug

A slug doesn't chew its food. It breaks it down with its tongue.

Most slugs feed on plants. They have a tongue with tiny teeth on it. When they lick their food, the teeth scrape off pieces for the slug to eat.

Slugs lay EGGS on top of the soil and under dead leaves. The eggs are covered in sticky slime to stop other minibeasts eating them.

Slug eggs look like little balls of jelly. A new slug grows inside each egg.

13

UNDER LOGS

When you walk in a wood or the countryside, look for logs on the ground. Some minibeasts live in or under logs.

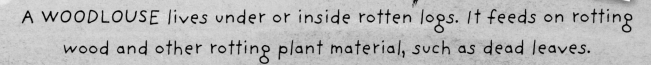

A WOODLOUSE lives under or inside rotten logs. It feeds on rotting wood and other rotting plant material, such as dead leaves.

A woodlouse has a suit of armour like an insect, but it belongs to a group of animals called **crustaceans** (*crus-tay-shuns*). It likes to stay in dark, damp places during the day. At night, as the **dew** falls, it searches for food on the woodland floor.

Tiny minibeasts called MITES can be found under logs. They hunt for springtails (see page 7). Mites have eight legs. They belong to the same group of animals as spiders.

Millipedes hide under logs, too. They sleep through the day and walk around to feed on dead plants at night. Just like the centipede, millipedes are arthropods with lots of legs.

WHAT CAN THIS BE?

A rolled up animal?
A pebble?
A berry?
Turn the page to find out.

It's a rolled up animal!

It's a PILL MILLIPEDE, curled up tightly into a ball. It is much shorter than the common millipede and has eighteen pairs of legs.

pill millipede

common millipede

There is a PILL WOODLOUSE, too. You can only tell it from the pill millipede when it uncurls and walks away. It only has seven pairs of legs.

Some wasp's nests look like a paper ball with a hole in the bottom.

WASPS are insects that visit old tree stumps. Some chew up pieces of rotten wood and take them away to make a nest. The nest may be under a leaf, in a hole in a wall or in a tree or bush.

Inside wasp nests are **cells**. A queen wasp lays an EGG in each one. When the egg hatches, the young grub is fed by other wasps until it turns into a pupa. An adult wasp hatches from the pupa.

Wasp grubs, and pupa (centre), live inside these hexagonal cells.

A wasp's stinger looks like a tiny needle at the end of its tail.

A wasp has a long, sharp point on its tail called a STING or stinger. It uses it to **defend** itself or kill other minibeasts. The stinger has **venom** in it that stops the **prey** animal from moving.

 Wasps can give you a painful sting. Keep away from wasp nests.

ON FLOWERS

Flowers attract different kinds of minibeasts. During spring and summer, BUTTERFLIES fly around flowers in gardens, parks and fields.

Butterfly WINGS are covered with lots of tiny **scales**. You need a microscope to see them.

Butterflies are insects. They feed on the **nectar** that plants make inside their flowers.

orange tip

common blue

red admiral

cabbage white

BEES are insects that fly around looking for brightly coloured flowers, too. When a bee lands on a flower, it feeds on the flower's nectar and collects **pollen** from the flower to take back to its nest.

There are many kinds of bees. Here are three of them.

red-tailed bumble bee

white-tailed bumble bee

honey bee

Pollen is spread among flowers by bees and sometimes by butterflies. This spreading of pollen helps flowers make seeds so they can make new flowers.

WHAT CAN THIS BE?

Soap bubbles?
An animal's home?
A bit of ice cream?
Turn the page to find out.

BUGS AND ANIMALS INSIDE PLANTS

It's an animal's home!

Inside the frothy bubbles is a SPITTLE BUG. It is the young stage of a bug called a froghopper.

spittle bug

Froghoppers can jump up to 70 cm high. They are named after frogs.

A spittle bug feeds on plant juices and makes froth to hide inside to keep safe. When it grows into an adult froghopper, it jumps to move about.

Bugs are a group of insects that have a mouth like a straw for sucking up liquids.

The meadow plant bug is long and thin. It likes to eat grass seeds.

The shield bug is named for the shape of its body.

If you look under a tree leaf you may find GREENFLY. They are tiny bugs that suck juice from leaves.

Some of the juice makes a thick, sticky liquid called honeydew.

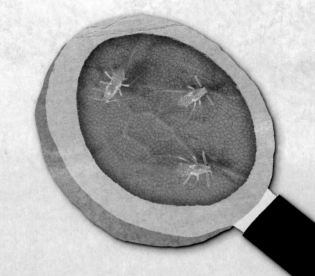

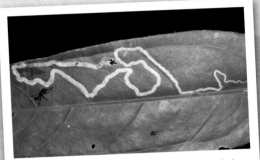

The wiggly line on this leaf is a tunnel made by a leaf miner.

Some small minibeasts live inside leaves. The LEAF MINER makes tunnels in leaves.

Tiny gall wasps make lumps on plants that their larvae live in. The lumps are called GALLS and some look a bit like a **wart**.

The nail gall is made by a mite. The mite lives inside the gall as it sucks juice from the leaf.

spangle gall

oak apple (gall)

nail gall

21

ON BUSHES AND TREES

Bushes and trees are also habitats for some minibeasts.

Low down in a bush is where SNAILS like to live. Snails are molluscs. They hide away inside their shells in the day. At night they move around to feed.

shell

eye

foot

Just like the slug, a snail moves along on its slimy foot and feeds on plants with its toothy tongue. Each long tentacle has an eye on the end of it.

On a branch of a bush or tree, you may find a type of beetle called a WEEVIL plodding along. It has a long **snout** that it uses to bite holes in plants to feed.

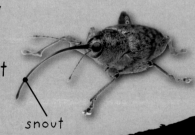

snout

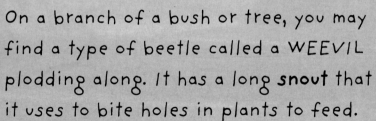

WATER SNAILS are molluscs that feed on **algae** and pond plants.

ramshorn snail

great pond snail

ear pond snail

water boatman

pond skater

The WATER BOATMAN feeds on algae and dead plants. It is very light and has long, hairy legs. It waves them about to stay near the water's surface.

The POND SKATER feeds on insects and spiders that fall in the water. Its long, hairy legs and light body help it walk on the water.

This colourful pond animal is about to fly away. What do you think it could be?

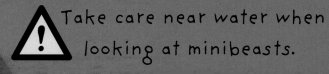

⚠️ Take care near water when looking at minibeasts.

MINIBEASTS CURIOSITY BOX

A curiosity box is a place to put all of the curious things you have collected.

What items are in your minibeasts curiosity box?

Slug and slime

Worm cast

Snail

Moth cocoon

Spider and web

CURIOUS QUIZ

1. Which is an armoured minibeast?
a) a slug
b) a woodlouse
c) an earthworm

2. What does a leatherjacket turn into?
a) a butterfly
b) a dragonfly
c) a crane fly

3. Which animal has two long and two short tentacles?
a) a slug
b) a maggot
c) a water boatman

4. What do wasps chew up to make nests?
a) spiders
b) stones
c) wood

5. What is a ruby tiger?
a) a big cat
b) a moth
c) a spider

6. Which animal has feelers like clubs?
a) an earwig
b) a butterfly
c) a harvestman

Curious quiz answers: 1b; 2c; 3a; 4c; 5b; 6b.
The colourful pond animal on page 27 is a dragonfly!

Pill millipede

Spittle bug froth

Caterpillar nibble holes

29

GLOSSARY

algae tiny plants that can join together to make green slime

arachnid an arthropod with eight legs

arthropod an animal with a hard skeleton of armour on the outside of its body

burrow a type of underground animal home

cell a small compartment

cocoon a case (or pupa) made by an insect larva to protect it as it turns into an adult

crustacean an arthropod that usually lives in water, such as a crab

defend an action to protect or stop an attack

dew water from the air that settles on the ground; it is usually seen on grass or plants

feeler a long, thin, bendy part on an animal's head that is used for touching and smelling

grain a tiny piece of rock that makes up soil

insect an animal with a hard body, six legs and usually two or four wings

larva a stage in the life cycle of some insects

limb a body part used for moving, such as a leg

mollusc an animal with a soft body and usually a shell, such as a snail or a clam

moult when an animal sheds feathers or skin

muscles parts of the body that allow it to move

nectar a sugary liquid made by some plants

pollen a yellow powder made by some flowers, which lets them make fruits and seeds

prey an animal that is eaten by other animals

pupa a stage in the life cycle of an insect where it changes from a larva to an adult

scales flat objects that overlap to cover something

shrimp a minibeast that is a crustacean

skeleton a part of the body that gives the whole body support and helps muscles move

snout a nose and mouth that is a long tube

tentacle a bendy body part that is carries an eye or is used to touch and grab

venom a poisonous liquid that animals use to kill prey or defend themselves

wart a hard lump that can form on human skin

CURIOUS FACTS

CURIOUS BEGINNINGS

People have collected objects for thousands of years. During the 1500s and 1600s, special cabinets were made to display the objects that were brought back from voyages to newly-discovered lands, such as North America. These cabinets were sometimes whole rooms, which became the first museums.

WHAT IS A CURIOSITY BOX?

A curiosity box is a small copy of these cabinets. It is a more scientific way of displaying items than a nature table. You can group items together by type or by theme. You may like to set up a curiosity box with photographs of living animals. Empty washed and cleaned snail shells, and leaves with tunnels or plant galls such as an oak apple could form real specimens to add to the photographs.

YOUR CURIOSITY BOX

It's easy to make your own curiosity box. A shoebox or other small cardboard box will do! Ask an adult to help you cut long strips of card with slits cut into them. Slot them together to make lots of small sections inside your box. Place the objects you find (or photographs of them) inside the sections.

USEFUL INFORMATION AND WEBLINKS

You can also set up containers of living minibeasts to be temporary curiosities. The tank or container you use must have air holes in the lid that are small enough so the animals can't escape. Return the minibeasts to where you found them after a few days.

Damp soil in a large plastic jar makes an excellent wormery. Add the worms and some vegetable food.

Slugs and snails are better housed in a small aquarium tank, with damp compost. Add the slugs or snails, and vegetables and fruit.

Woodlice and pill woodlice can also be set up in a small aquarium tank. Add damp compost, moss and a rotting log.

Explore the website of Buglife, the charity working to save minibeasts worldwide: www.buglife.org.uk

Join the Bug Club to find out how to keep some invertebrates: www.amentsoc.org/bug-club/

For information on practical science involving plants and animals, contact the Association for Science Education at www.ase.org.uk for their book *Be Safe!* (Fourth edition).

MINIBEASTS NOTES

Here is some more information, for parents and teachers, on the minibeasts and habitats found in this book.

What are minibeasts?

Minibeasts are all around us. In this book the reader is introduced to common habitats and the minibeasts that live there. It is possible to visit examples of these habitats within a city park where there may be a flower garden, un-mown wild areas, a pond, bushes and trees.

The term 'minibeasts' is used to make animals also known as 'creepy crawlies' more attractive for study by young children. It is not a biological grouping, but all these animals are invertebrates. Minibeasts are an important part of food chains. They are food for many species of mammals, birds, reptiles, amphibians and fish, and even humans!

The armour-like skeleton on the outside of some minibeasts' bodies is called an exoskeleton. Earthworms, slugs and snails have a hydrostatic skeleton. This is formed from water that is trapped in cavities in the body. The water forms a material that gives support to the body's muscles.

In the soil

There are several kinds of springtail. They all have an extra limb held close to the underside of the body, which they can extend rapidly to generate a force that springs them away from predators.

Earthworms belong to the annelid group, whose bodies are made of a series of rings. The head end is more pointed than the tail end. The underside has rows of stiff bristles, which can be gently felt with a finger. These bristles help the earthworm grip the soil to help it move.

Under stones

The earwig is not a beetle. It belongs to an insect group called dermaptera. During an earwig's life cycle, a small version of the adult (nymph) hatches from an egg. As it grows it moults its skin. At the final moult it acquires wings and reproductive organs, and becomes an adult.

Centipedes don't have one hundred legs. Many have fewer and some have more. To tell a centipede from a millipede, look at how many pairs of legs are attached to each body segment. Centipedes have one pair per segment and millipedes *seem* to have two. In reality, millipedes also have one pair per segment, but each exoskeleton plate covers two segments.

Under logs

Woodlice are crustaceans – an animal group that includes crabs. The exoskeleton of insects is watertight, but the exoskeleton of the woodlouse isn't. This means that woodlice hide in damp places during the day, so they don't dry out. At night, when dew falls and the air is damp, they come out. For a woodlouse, the dew falling is like the tide coming in for a crab.

Millipedes do not have a thousand legs. The largest number of legs found on a millipede is 750. Millipedes and centipedes belong to the invertebrate group called myriapods. Although the pill millipede and pill woodlouse show the same features, they are not closely related. The pill millipede is a myriapod and the pill woodlouse is a crustacean. The pill woodlouse is also known as the common pill bug or roly poly.

Wasp nests are made from a mixture of chewed up wood fibres and wasp saliva. It is made by species of social wasps. Solitary wasps do not make nests. **Wasps can be dangerous. Never disturb their nests.**

On flowers

Butterflies are mainly seen from the spring to the autumn, but the red admiral can be seen at any time of year. Not all bees live in colonies; some bees are solitary. Butterflies and bees are important pollinators of flowers. They are attracted to flowers by their colour and scent and move pollen grains from flower to flower as they feed on nectar.

Bugs, and animals inside plants

The term 'bugs' is often used for all kinds of minibeasts. The term is correctly used to describe a group within the insect group, called the hemiptera, or true bugs. The characteristic feature of a true bug is mouth parts fused into a tube for sucking liquids. Many bugs suck plant juices, but some, like the bed bug, suck blood.

Greenfly (also called aphids) are bugs. They pierce a plant and suck its juices. As the juice is low in nutrients, the greenfly have to feed on lots of it.

Minibeasts that burrow into plants for part of their life cycle leave evidence of their presence as tunnels. They may also cause the invaded plant to grow a structure round them called a gall, which provides food and shelter for them. Galls can be a variety of shapes, sizes and colours.

On bushes and trees

Snails 'roost' together during the day. At night they roam around the area to feed before returning to their 'roost'. The slime that slugs and snails produce is called mucus. Snails also use it to seal themselves in their shells during dry weather to stop their bodies dehydrating. The dried mucus produces a skin, called an epiphragm across the shell opening.

Caterpillars of each species of moth or butterfly feed on certain plants know as their food plants. For example the food plant of the red admiral is the common nettle. Moths usually fly at night and butterflies fly by day.

Not all spiders spin webs. Wolf spiders run around on the ground and can usually be seen if an area of grassy ground is watched for a few minutes. The harvestman is slow moving, so its pair of eyes, which are on a turret on top of its body, are worth examining with a magnifying glass.

Streams and ponds

The movement of the water creates different habitats. In flowing water, the minibeasts are adapted to hold their place, either using a sucker (river limpet) or by hiding under stones (freshwater shrimp).

Still water gives plants a chance to put down roots and grow, which in turn provides food for snails. Slow swimming insects, such as the backswimmer, can thrive here too. A force called surface tension makes the water surface behave as if it is covered in a weak skin. A pond skater spreads out its weight on feet set wide apart so it can stand on the 'skin'. **Children visiting water habitats must always be supervised by an adult.**